Starting Your First Potted Vegetable Garden

How to create a garden oasis

(A Guide)

E. Hughes

Love-LovePublishing—Madison, WI
Paperback ISBN: 978-1-961823-30-3
Hardcover ISBN: 978-1-961823-31-0
Library of Congress Control Number: 2025937919
Title: *Starting Your First Potted Vegetable Garden*
Author: E. Hughes
Formats | Hardcover and Paperback Editions
Genre: Non-Fiction
Subject: Gardening

Hardcover : *A Coffee Table Book*
Paperback: *A Guide*

ABOUT THE BOOK

Learn how to grow your own potted vegetable garden in this informative coffee table book by E. Hughes. This book is for first-time gardeners interested in growing a beautiful potted or container garden in a small or large space, whether on your patio or backyard. Join the growing lifestyle trend of container gardening to add feng shui and tranquility to your space.

Make your home even more fabulous with great tips sure to help you get started and provide you with the lush garden your heart desires, even if you lack a green thumb. You can enjoy flowers and vibrant hearty fruits and vegetables, right on your own patio or porch. You can grow them in pots and gift your friends, families, and guests with some of the best homegrown fruits and vegetables they have ever had.

This book includes tips on identifying types of gardening pests, the best time of year to garden, the easiest vegetables to grow, easy planting tips, and information on hydroponic (indoor) gardening.

ABOUT THE AUTHOR

E. Hughes is the author of *Reality Unbound: The Digital Mind and the Nature of Reality.* She is also the author of *Space, Time, and Loneliness (A Poetry Chapbook), Time and the Multi-Universe: A philosophy of time and time travel, Sixth Iteration, Digital Smiles, Beyond the Plain, Disappear, Love, A Mediterranean Romance, The Sapphire Chronicles, The Penelope children's book series, and more.*

Learn more about the author via her official website, https://ehughesbooks.com

INTRODUCTION

*S*tarting *Your First Potted Vegetable Garden: How to create a garden oasis,* is a simple guide to help novice gardeners plant their first container or potted garden, whether you are growing vegetables, fruit or regular plants. This is an expanded version of my book, *Starting Your First Patio Garden: A Coffee book.*

When I started my first garden, I looked at many DIY websites and books and found some of the plans were too sophisticated for my modest little townhouse. The layouts were sunlit, gorgeous, and intimidating.

I was a city girl living in a contained, but bustling high-traffic part of town and the area where my garden would be planted was merely a small patio enclosed by a tall wooden fence. How do I start a garden with this? Then I realized my garden didn't have to look sophisticated, or fancy like the ones on the DIY websites or books. I could do whatever I wanted, as long as I could get my plants to grow. I discovered my love of gardening in 2007 after an impulse purchase of a small tomato plant at a grocery store. I watered it every day. It sat outside on my partially shaded doorstep for about a month, before it started to bear fruit. I was amazed that I could grow anything, let alone a tomato. I went to the store and purchased another. That year, I grew two tomato plants on my patio.

The following year, I grew an entire garden in large $10 container pots. It was small, but effective. Tomatoes, bell peppers, cilantro, parsley, basil, and an eggplant (that I had planted in a Topsy Turvey Tomato Planter) had grown beautifully that year. When friends visited, their mouths dropped. I knew I had achieved something, when one day at six in the morning, I looked out my window to find my neighbor, a little ninety year-old lady from Mexico with a blade standing on my patio, cutting cilantro. I never used cilantro, and the stalks had grown taller than I was, and had grown flowers that sprouted seeds. I had invited some of my neighbors to pluck a tomato any time they wanted. I smiled, and closed the curtains as she slowly walked back to her townhouse. I continued to grow a garden every year, adding different varieties of tomatoes while experimenting with the different types of vegetables I could grow in pots. The photos in this book are from 2009-2024. The photos from 2009 show images from my second floor patio garden. The 2015 images show my garden outside of my townhouse. My garden with the large backyard shows my garden as it exists in 2024. My gardens are never overly fancy or elaborate. I'm not striving for perfection, except in the quality of my fruits and vegetables. Sometimes my patio or backyard (filled with supplies, dirt or even cracks between the concrete) can look a little beat up, except with large, beautiful green plants that make the entire area look vibrant, gorgeous, and lush. I've added trickling fountains, trellises covered in flowers and vegetables, and wonderful displays of nature all around. I grow a wild garden these days. With this book, I did not want to go the fancy route or for perfection. Sometimes, when we see something that looks a bit out of reach, we don't follow through. It's a creative process but new gardeners shouldn't feel pressured to grow a garden that looks like it's out of the pages of a "Better Homes and Garden" magazine (though you can if you want!) The idea is to add special touches from fountains, rocks, or any landscaping idea that works for you and your home, no matter how large or small your garden area will be. I hope you enjoy the book.

- E. Hughes

Table of Contents

GARDEN SMARTER, NOT HARDER

Gardening has given me such joy that I wrote a guide for people who are interested in growing a garden but have little to zero gardening experience, limited space, a busy career, family, limited time or budget. You may even want a patio table and chairs as a nice shady space for your guests to sip tea or coffee where you might talk about the fresh roses, or the tomatoes growing around you. In this book I will show you how to start a beautiful and productive garden. It doesn't need to be fancy or elaborate. Every gardener and garden is different.

Tip: *Add flowers to what may become a bland green vegetable garden. The splash of color will brighten your patio, enhancing this rich green space.* Breathe life into your space. Don't be afraid of an eclectic mix of color.

Dull pots and lack of flowers can create a bland patio space even when your growth is lush. Try adding a splash of color like flowers or colorful pots. Growing a garden is not only about producing fruits, vegetables, or flowers, but having a serene place to retreat; a private garden oasis smack in the middle of the city in your backyard, your patio or porch. Potted gardens can be elaborate or modest, it depends on the person. I have had big and small gardens, depending on the year. Even with a big yard, I prefer to grow as much as I can in a small amount of space, while someone else might prefer only a few plants or flowers in small pots. So...where do you begin?

This book is by no means, a comprehensive scientific guide to gardening. But it will have important tips and guidance for new gardeners. It is in short, an overview of what to expect, how to get it started, and how to keep your garden growing for the duration of summer. We're going to take a few shortcuts to starting your first vegetable garden and it's going to look fabulous!

2 - Vibrant tomato and bell pepper plants

(Note: There are huge online garden communities on social media platforms like Tiktok, Instagram, and even Facebook, where people share photos and videos of their beautiful container gardens. Potted gardens have become more popular.)

The pots above are fairly large in size and hold two to three tomato or bell pepper plants. There is an onion plant, and the small square grey pot has four strawberry plants. Strawberry plants are beautiful but can be tricky to grow. Especially as you will begin to grow daughter plants from them, and should remove the daughter plants and plant them elsewhere so that they don't pull resources from the rest of the plant.

3 Starter vegetable plants (Newly planted cir. 2009)

So how do you start a garden? Let's start with the easy stuff, then work our way to more complex gardening, like planting from a seed.

What type of vegetables do I recommend for a first time gardener?

1. Tomatoes
2. Cucumbers
3. Bell Peppers
4. Jalapenos
5. Lettuce

These are the least complicated vegetable plants to grow when you are planting your first garden. The image above shows that you can grow a garden even on a small second-floor patio. For people who live in housing that lack a patio or backyard, you may want an indoor hydroponic garden, which I will get to later.

What you will need:

Gardening tools, potting or gardening soil, seeds, pots, containers, and/or an in-ground or above-ground garden bed.

Supplies:

1.   You will need a bag of compost (Unless you prefer ready-made gardening or potting soil, like Miracle Grow). Compost is comprised of leaves, twigs, and other decomposed organic material from plants, and dirt. You might find brands like Root Organics useful among many other brands. Compost is useful for people who wish to grow organic fruit. In this case you want to exclude regular gardening soil that may "feed" plants for several months.

2. **Since I grow my garden in pots or an elevated garden bed instead of directly in the ground, I prefer to use potting soil** like *Miracle Grow Potting Soil for Flowers and Vegetables*. *Vigoro* is also a great brand. So don't buy any kind of soil, make sure that it is specific to growing vegetables if you plan to grow fruit or vegetables. Try to find potting soil that will feed your plants for the duration of the season. I prefer potting soil that will feed the plants for 6 to 9 months.

3. Pots. You'll want big pots, 18-21 inches. If you can find an even bigger pot, get one. The bigger the pot, the bigger the fruit. Smaller pots don't

yield much fruit, if any at all. You can find inexpensive 18 to 21 inch pots at Home Depot or Wal-Mart, for example.

4. If you have rabbits or creatures in your yard, look for a raised garden bed. You can find them at Amazon, Home Depot, Lowes or your local garden nursery.

5. Water and lots of it. Use a hose or a bucket of clean water that's not too hot or too cold. Use tepid or room temperature water.

6. You'll need starter plants or seeds. A starter plant is a seed that has already grown or sprouted into a small plant.

7. Garden tools like a trowel, to help you dig a hole in the dirt where you will insert the base of your starter plant or seed. The tools pictured on page 4 are perfect for a potted garden. You can buy starter plants or grow them a month or two before you plant your garden outdoors.

How to plant a potted garden

(A wall of starter plants at a retail gardening center)

1. I live in the Midwest where we have very cold winters. Here, you must plant after the threat of frost is over. This is usually by mid-April. Depending on the hardiness zone you live in, dates when it is safe to start gardening outdoors can vary. It is usually safe to plant outdoors by mid-spring. In warmer climates, you can usually plant year-round.

2. Build your garden bed, or arrange your pots the way you would like them on your patio, back porch, or backyard. They will be heavy once filled with soil so you should move them into position before pouring your soil into the pots or garden bed. You will want very large 18-21" pots.

3. Pour the soil into your pot, container, or garden until it is completely filled, only an inch or two away from the top. You don't want your soil so low that your plant or seed may not get enough sunlight. The soil will also shrink or sink a little after it is wet for the first time.

4. Dig a hole about the depth of your starter plant. Remove the wrapper and plastic cup. Bury only the soil part of the starter plant. Do not bury the entire

plant. Gently loosen the soil a bit to give the roots room.

5. Plant two or three per large plant pot or container or one or two in a smaller pot.

6. After burying your plant, cover the hole with dirt. Remember, you are only burying the dirt at the bottom of your starter plant.

(Starter plants before planting)

7. Place something under your pot to catch water if you have a patio that is above ground and neighbors below.

8. In an 18-21" pot, you can plant up to 3 to 4 starter plants, set a decent distance apart in one large pot. A smaller pot should have only one or two plants.

9. Water your plant, but do not overwater. The soil should not look like mud.
10.   Then start on your next pot, fill with dirt, and repeat steps 1 through 7.

Be sure you are getting at least 6 to 8 hours of sunlight per day. On those scorching hot 90 degree Fahrenheit / 32 degree Celsius or higher days, you may need to water your plants twice. Do not let your soil become dry unless it's a plant that does not require a lot of watering, like a succulent. If your soil is too moist, it will slowly drown your plant. So make sure that you don't see stagnant water that doesn't seem to get absorbed into your soil or soil that always looks like mud. Your leaves will turn yellow and look wilted if they are overwatered. They will wilt or turn yellow or brown if under-watered.

After planting your starter plants into large pots, the plants will appear small, but will grow quickly depending on how well nourished they are. If you are using a potting soil that includes plant food, or you are providing the proper nourishment for your plant through the compost or natural plant foods, and watering your plants every day, except on days when there is rain, and the plant is given plenty of sunshine, within two three weeks, you will see tremendous growth.

(Starter plants make starting a potted garden easier for new gardeners. Over time, you'll likely graduate to planting your own seeds after you have mastered growing big lush green productive plants from tiny starter plants. Despite starting from a young seedling, it is still your hard work that brings it to life and fosters its growth. So in the beginning, grow smarter, not harder.)

(After 2 1/2 weeks of growth)

The potted starter plants above have doubled in size two weeks after planting, mostly due to rainwater, which seems to grow plants faster. I hope for significant rain during spring as vegetable plants will grow better than it does using water from tap, or watering through your garden hose. Rainwater is the best! Of course, you will use both. You will need to water daily except on days when it rains, as overwatering will devastate your plant.

I recommend starter plants because it can take a few weeks for seeds to germinate and sprout into seedling when weather is reasonable. Sometimes insects and even chipmunks or squirrels will eat your seeds or seedlings before they have had a chance to sprout or grow into a full plant. Otherwise, first time gardeners can also grow their seeds indoors two months ahead of planting season to avoid this issue.

Seeds are inexpensive. You can also use seeds from veggies that you buy from the store, but keep in mind those seeds may be genetically altered or may not grow properly. It is also okay to use seeds from plants that you have grown in your own garden. Starter plants are also usually inexpensive, particularly for a small garden like mine. The price ranges from only a couple of dollars per plant. Vegetable plants that are fully grown and bearing fruit have a higher cost.

The image below features the same plants that are displayed on pages 9 and 10. This is after three to four weeks of growth. Notice that the tomatoes are already growing. If you take care of your plant, ensure that your soil has plenty of plant food, water, sunlight, and warm weather and your vegetables will grow quickly.

The importance of hardiness zones

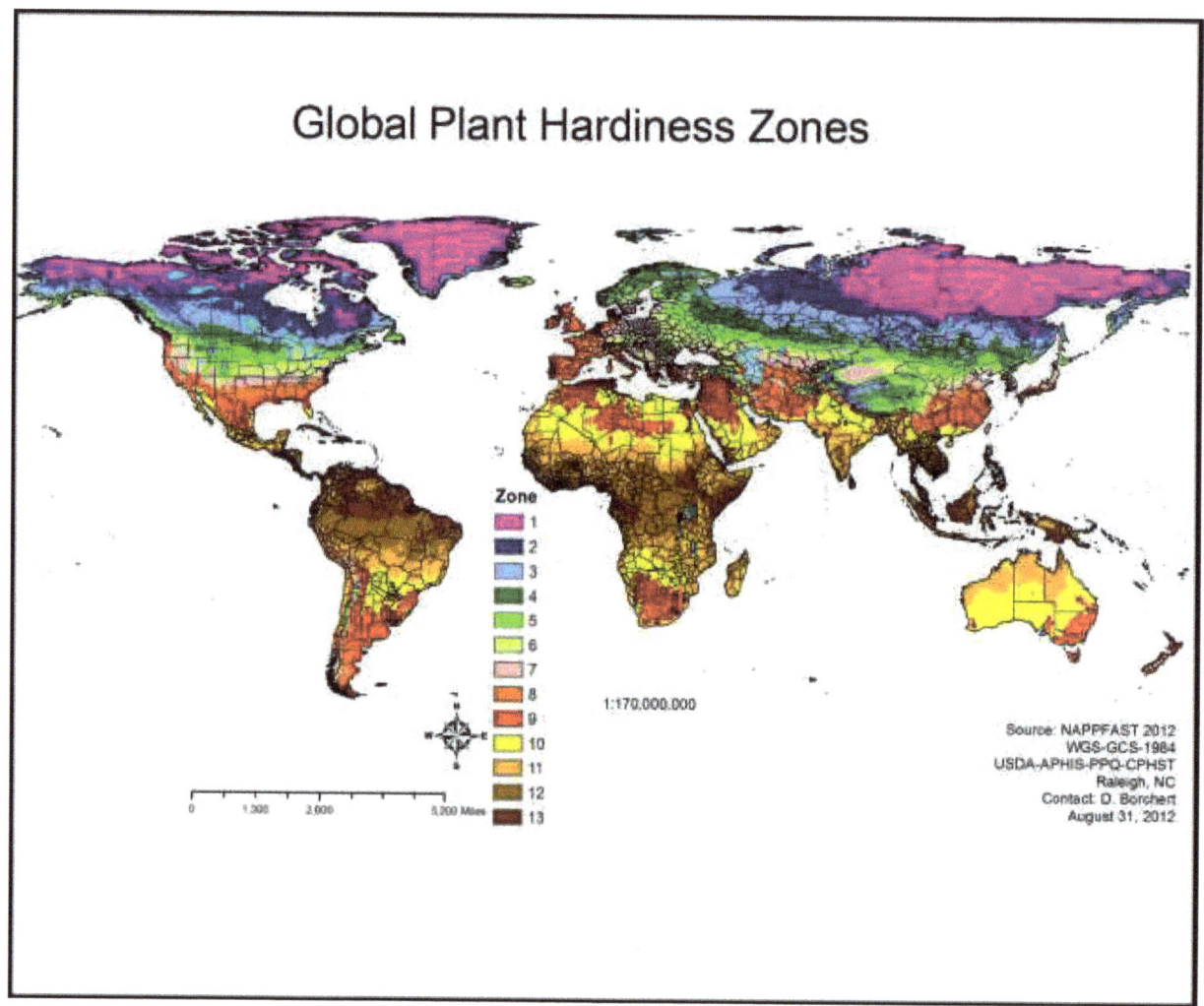

Domain, https://commons.wikimedia.org/w/index.php?curid=83615430

The illustration above shows a global map of hardiness zones. The colors correspond to each region's temperature range during the winter.

When you should plant your garden will vary based on the hardiness zone assigned to where you live. In colder climates, usually when the first frost has passed. For gardeners who live in warm climates, you can safely plant year-round, although, certain fruits and vegetables will thrive better depending on the time of year. For example, leafy vegetables like lettuce and kale will grow better during fall or early spring (they are not at their best in hot weather). In the Midwest, you would plant garlic in the fall and let it grow throughout winter and harvest late spring.

What planting/garden zone are you in?

The numbers on the chart below correspond to regional planting zones by temperature. The importance of this chart is to help gardeners determine the type of plants they can grow and what time of year to plant them. The USDA divides North America into 13 zones based on winter temperature lows.

Average Annual Extreme Minimum Temperature 1976-2005

Temp (F)	Zone	Temp (C)
-60 to -50	1	-51.1 to -45.6
-50 to -40	2	-45.6 to -40
-40 to -30	3	-40 to -34.4
-30 to -20	4	-34.4 to -28.9
-20 to -10	5	-28.9 to -23.3
-10 to 0	6	-23.3 to -17.8
0 to 10	7	-17.8 to -12.2
10 to 20	8	-12.2 to -6.7
20 to 30	9	-6.7 to -1.1
30 to 40	10	-1.1 to 4.4
40 to 50	11	4.4 to 10
50 to 60	12	10 to 15.6
60 to 70	13	15.6 to 21.1

You can grow your vegetable and fruit trees in certain zones. It's important to know which zone you live in based on your state or country. See the chart on the left or the Global Hardiness Map on page 8 for your country.

I live in Zone 5b. This means certain plants will not thrive in this zone year-round due to cold winters. You can plant in late spring after the final frost and care for your gardens during spring and summer. Some plants, like garlic can be planted in the fall and harvested in the spring. In this zone, I can't grow lemon trees or citrus fruits outdoors. Although, I have grown lemon trees in indoor pots and placed them outside during spring and summer months.

Image credit:
By USDA-ARS and Oregon State University (OSU) - USDA Agricultural Research Service (USDA-ARS), Public Domain, https://commons.wikimedia.org/w/index.php?curid=69681699

Did you know? You can grow potatoes from store bought potatoes? First, store a few potatoes in a cool dark cabinet. Check your potatoes for "eyes". These are the little green sprouts that grow from potatoes when they start to get old. You can plant them in soil with the sprouts/eyes poking out of the soil. Do not bury the spouts. Your potato does not need to be buried deeply. You can use a grow bag or a large pot. Do not crowd them together for bigger potatoes.

You can grow sweet potatoes using the slips. These are the plants that grow from a sweet potato. You can use the slips to grow hundreds of new sweet potatoes. Just cut the plants off at the base of the stalk or even cut from the vine growing from your sweet potato plants and plant the individual slips directly in soil. Grow in very warm to hot weather.

First, you will need to determine what type of gardener you are. I try to be an environmentally conscious gardener, at least, as much as I can be. I observe movements like, *"No, Mow May,"* which is when gardeners avoid mowing their grass during the month of May to support the ecosystem. *No Mow May* gives insects like butterflies and bees time to pollinate flowers. I also prefer to grow a wild garden. Some gardeners prefer to stake their tomato vines, trim leaves, or completely strip all of the leaves off of their tomatoes, trim the hedges and rose bushes, and have manicured lawns. I prefer to let my vegetables grow into big wild vines or

bushes. There has been an ongoing trend to grow "wild" or "rewilding" to support biodiversity and to end the overuse of valuable resources like the water that we use when watering our lawns. However, there are downsides to the trend that I will get to later.

Grow lights

As mentioned earlier, the best time to plant outdoors is when the threat of frost has passed. If you are planting from seeds, I recommend planting your seeds indoors a month or two earlier under a special grow-light (which is a lamp that simulates sunlight) or start your planting early in a greenhouse so that your plants are already growing when it is time to plant your garden outdoors in the spring. These will basically become your starter plants, like the ones that you can purchase from a retailer, except you are growing them on your own. A glow-light can be used for both indoor gardens or in greenhouses.

How do you know when your fruit or vegetables are ready to grow?

You will know when your vegetables or fruit are ready to grow when flowers appear on your vegetable plants. This is when bees and other pollinators become important, since they transfer pollen to your flowers, allowing them to produce. If your vegetable plant grows flowers but does not produce fruit or vegetable, you may need to use a vibrating toothbrush or a pollinator brush to manually pollinate your flowers by spreading pollination from one flower to another. Pollen typically looks like a very fine dust. Manual pollination is usually effective when done right. Otherwise, nature will do what it needs to do for you, as insects like butterflies, bees, and moths will transfer the pollen from flower to flower as these pollinating insects look for nectar and food.

Closer look: In the image on page 16, you can see cucumbers slowly growing from the stem connected to the yellow flower. Where the stem appears slightly thicker, are very tiny cucumbers! Flowers can be white, yellow, or other colors. On page 18, in the square pot there are four peanut plants. Funny story...when I planted peanuts for the first time, I was annoyed that I did not see any peanuts growing. Turns out, they grow below the soil. Root vegetables and legumes do not need pollination.

In this image: Square pot *(above right)*, four peanut plants, second square pot; four bell pepper plants, round pots are various tomato plants, 2 per pot. You don't want too many tomato plants in one pot. 3 is the max for medium-large pots. Distance is important. Over time, your garden will grow. But you will need to water them every day. **Do not miss a day unless it rains.** With plenty of fresh water, your plant will grow tall and bear plenty of fruit.

Growing tomato and bell pepper plants on a hot dry day

How to grow a garden from seeds

Growing a vegetable plant from seed is fairly straightforward. You will need to buy seeds and plant them in a small planter or harvest seeds from a mature plant if you are skilled enough. Your soil will need food and nutrients so you will need to invest in plant food. As I mentioned earlier, you can use compost for an organic garden or perhaps Miracle Grow potting soil for fruits and vegetables. The best place to grow your seedling is outdoors where it will get plenty of sunlight. However, animals and insects will often eat the seeds before they grow. As a result, many gardeners will grow their seedlings indoor until the plant has grown a few inches, before planting them outside in the ground or in a pot.

Biodegradable peat pots for seedlings will work best, though you can use a regular or plastic planter. Peat pots can be square-shaped or round. There are also peat pot starter trays. You will need to fill of the peat pots with soil then plant your seed. Your seed pack will tell you how deep to plant your seeds. You can then grow them under a grow light until the seedling sprouts. During the germination period, you will need to cover it with a clear top, which is similar to creating a mini greenhouse for each plant. When you see the little seedling push through the soil, you can remove the plastic cover and continue to let it grow. Because so many vegetable plants have different timeframes for germination, and there isn't a standard time for most plants, I will not list germination times here. The range is 1 to 4 weeks, depending on the plant. Your seed packet will also tell you how long it will take for the seed germinate.

Types of garden beds

There are different types of garden beds to choose from. There are raised garden beds, in which the garden is elevated from the ground in a wood or metal box. There are raised garden beds/pots with legs (see pg. 19). These are useful in keeping rabbits from reaching your vegetables. Then there are large planting pots like the ones you've seen in some of the earlier photos, and then there are grow bags. Grow bags can be plastic but are mostly cloth. Some are great for growing root vegetables like potatoes and come with a small opening on the side of the bag to help retrieve your vegetables. Root vegetables are vegetables that grow below the soil, like carrots or potatoes.

The stock photo above shows potato plants in a grow bag. Some grow bags are green, can be black, brown, plastic or cloth. The image on the next page shows a raised garden bed with legs, which we used to grow mini-egg plants.

The image above shows one of my garden beds, which I used with a trellis. This is shortly after the flowers were planted. In the garden bed on the other side, I planted cucumber and pepper plants. The cucumber vines and flowers eventually grew up the trellis, covering it completely.

You can grow lettuce broccoli, eggplant, and many other vegetables in a raised garden bed.

Tip: When you water plants, aim your water at the soil to ensure you reach the roots.

How to grow an indoor hydroponic garden

Hydroponic gardening is when you grow plants in water without soil. There are a number of new inexpensive hydroponic gardening systems that you can acquire from retailers, many starting at about $60 USD. A hydroponic garden uses a small grow sponge which is where you will plant the seed. The sponge is inserted into a slot in the hydroponic device. A tub at the bottom of the device is filled with water and requires liquid plant food that will feed the root system, allowing the plants to grow. It's less complicated than it sounds. What's great about hydroponic gardening is that plants and vegetables grow faster than it does in soil. The downside is that your vegetables may be smaller, depending on the size of the hydroponic garden. On the upside, a large hydroponic garden device will produce normal-sized to small produce.

Hydroponic Garden and seedlings
Note: Seedlings are growing out of grow sponges.

The easiest vegetables to grow in a hydroponic garden are tomatoes, lettuce, peppers, and herbs. Some hydroponic devices have grow lamps that are fairly tall in height, allowing you to grow vegetables that are tall, like tomato vines or bell pepper plants. For hydroponic gardens that have shorter grow lamps, you will find that it is easy to grow different varieties of lettuce or herbs. Some people use their hydroponic gardens to grow a beautiful array of flowers. In the end, you can take your garden to the dinner table, and even use cut and regrow methods for your lettuce. This means, after harvesting your lettuce, don't pull them completely. You can cut them two inches above the stem and the lettuce will regrow without having to plant new seeds. You can cycle your cut and regrow multiple times before starting over and replanting with a new seed.

The most important vegetable to grow in your garden, whether indoors or outdoors will be tomatoes. When picking seeds or starter plants, check whether your tomatoes will be determinate or indeterminate. I prefer indeterminate because they grow all summer long while determinate tomatoes will grow only a limited number of tomatoes. Determinate will grow in bunches while indeterminate will grow along the vine. Determinate tomatoes typically ripen at the same time in a short amount of time while indeterminate tomatoes are constantly growing and ripening throughout the season.

Lettuce and tomatoes growing in different hydroponic gardens. Top right image shows the root system of growing plants.

Accessories

How you design your garden is completely up to you. Your garden doesn't have to look perfect, or like something out of a magazine. I want my garden to feel serene, peaceful, and lush. Accessories like garden statues and fountains can add beauty to a garden. On Mother's Day, I was gifted a beautiful trickling fountain by my daughter. It was a large stone fountain with a functional water mill so there's always the sound of trickling water, and birds chirping in the garden. The year before, I made a DIY solar fountain using a barrel of water. Making or buying decorations can add spark to your garden. I like turtles, frogs, and sunflowers. I also use less attractive but practical props like cinder blocks to keep my vegetables out of the reach of rabbits or our local woodchuck. The image below was taken by my security camera, during No Mow May in 2024. Each year, I try to do something different or add something new.

A trellis is also useful as both an aesthetic and as a place to grow your flowers and vegetables. Here, we grew Climatis, a climbing flower, on the left side and cucumbers and peppers on the right. The vines from the Climatis and cucumbers grew to the top of the trellis by the end of summer. There's lots of planting and building involved and help needed when pouring soil. I could not have succeeded without help from family. Without them, this would have been a much smaller garden. The image on pg 29 shows my garden in 2025. This year, I focused on aesthetics and added more flowers, which includes a double double rose tree, begonias, and added dragon breath and celosia to the garden bed. For the vegetables, I grew 20 tomato plants, a variety of hot peppers, cucumbers, bell peppers, sweet potatoes, and potatoes.

Common garden pests

The most important way to deal with common garden pests is to identify them early. Pests include animals (rabbits, squirrels, woodchucks, raccoons), insects, fungus, blights, disease and other infestations. Pests are common in gardening.

The most frustrating gardening pests, and they are difficult to avoid, are aphids and spider mites. They are not dangerous to humans, but they do ruin your plants. Spider mites are tiny, and almost imperceptible to the eye. They suck the sap out of your plants and infect your entire garden if not treated, or if the plant is not isolated right away. If you see little bugs, swarms of them crawling all over your soil, they are likely spider mites. Ants and other insects are expected, especially outdoors, but you'll know you have spider mites when your plants begin to turn yellow, brown, and wither. You'll want to treat your plants with peppermint spray, and isolate it so that other plants are not infected. Aphids are annoying, gross, but harmless. You can blast them off your plant with water from a water hose, and they will go away. Aphids are tiny jumping/flying insects, and there are so many of them they can cover entire leaves and stalks. There are also fuzzy aphids. These are white and fluffy and can look like tiny bits of pollen. A good blast of water will get rid of them as well. Fungus is also a problem. You will know your plants are infected if they are covered by a white powdery dust, like the pumpkin plant on pg 30. The fungus did not show up until the end of summer. Everything must be cleaned if you don't want the fungus to return next year. I did not keep the pumpkins. You can see the healthy pumpkin plant before and after the fungal infection. If you see a spot on your plant, remove it early. Don't wait for it to spread. Cut the entire branch or leaf. **Blight and blossom rot** is often due to calcium deficiencies. You can remedy this by putting crushed eggshells in your soil.

One of the most dangerous gardening pests is an invasive tree called Common Buckthorn. It releases a chemical into the ground called Emodin to inhibit surrounding plant growth to outcompete other species of plants. I lost two apple trees in 2024. For the past two or three years, I noticed that several trees had died. One tree fell on its own but thankfully it was small and did not cause any damage. Then in 2024, one of our two apple trees died, and had to be removed. The other died and simply fell on its own, even though it had grown a lot of apples that were nearly ready to harvest. I also noticed the overgrowth of ground ivy instead of grass, is also an invasive species.

The grass wasn't growing as well. I believe in growing wild, but there seemed to be something odd about what was happening. It was as though the ecosystem was slowly dying. While on a walk through the yard, all the way to the other end, I discovered several trees growing dark brown/purple-ish berries. I took a picture of it and uploaded it to a plant identifier website, and learned it was a Common Buckthorn tree. This suddenly explained everything. There was one growing next to where the apple trees were, one growing in front of the house, and two in the middle of the yard. The invasive trees were destroying the ecosystem. The yard is still recovering. Common Buckthorn must be removed and the stump poisoned to keep it from growing back or it will return. The berries are also highly poisonous. Thank goodness I did not eat them. I also have a cherry tree and the berries look very similar.

Common Buckthorn berries and leaves (L)   Fallen apple tree (R)

A tip for getting rid of aphids are lady bugs, a natural predator to the aphid insect. Some gardeners will bring lady bugs into their garden to get rid of aphids. The imbalance caused by the Common Buckthorn tree, led to excessive ground ivy, weeds, and even pests like fungus. This invasive species of tree is not native to North America so its spread often goes unchecked. The yard is still recovering.

The image below shows a healthy pumpkin plant and the same pumpkin plant infected by a fungus later. You'll notice white spots on the leaves.

Healthy Cucumber (L) and diseased cucumber (R)

Happier gardening tips

One essential tool that every gardener should have is a lettuce knife. Lettuce knives are plastic rather than metal but are very sharp. When you cut your vegetables with metal, your vegetables will turn brown at the edges from oxidation caused by the metal. To prevent premature oxidation and browning of your vegetables or fruit, use a lettuce knife instead of a regular metal knife. Some lettuce knives can be ceramic.

Lettuce is the fastest and easiest vegetable to grow. Lettuce will grow better in warm weather, and does not grow as well in really hot weather. You want to grow your lettuce in early spring and in the fall when temperatures are moderate. Vegetables like Brussels sprouts and broccoli also grow better in early spring and fall in moderate temperatures. For example, during consistently scorching hot summer days, broccoli will sometimes "bolt." Bolting is when a vegetable plant matures prematurely and is not considered a viable produce. Instead of producing a broccoli head it will flower and a produce seeds. When cutting broccoli, use a lettuce knife and cut at an angle if you plan to grow broccoli shoots after the main broccoli head is cut. A broccoli shoot is a small broccoli sprout that grows after the main broccoli has been produced and cut. Typically, you only get one main broccoli head from this plant.

Onions: Onions grow and have long green stalks. The onion bulb grows below the soil and the green stalk above. The green stalk is actually a green onion and is edible. Your yellow, Vidalia/sweet onion, or white onion will be ready to harvest when your green onion stalks lay flat instead of upright.

Tomatoes are always green until they turn ripe. You can sometimes eat green tomatoes, but make sure they are very close to ripe and close to turning red. Tomatoes are part of the Nightshade family so deeply green tomatoes can cause sickness, so don't eat too many. Some tomatoes are black, like Black Cherokee or Black Prince Tomatoes by Bonnie Plants. These are delicious! Some plants are yellow, like Lemon Boy (my absolute favorite tomato) or Yellow Jubilee.

Tip: Some of your vegetables could have imperfections. Some of the imperfections that can occur when growing tomatoes are cracks and splitting. This happens when the tomato plant hasn't been watered and is suddenly watered. The tomato swells, and then splits down the middle. These are sometimes ruined, so be sure to water your plants daily, especially when it's hot.

(Black Prince and Early Girl tomatoes)

Beefsteak, Lemon Boy, Early Girl, Heirloom, with bell peppers

Bring tranquility to your garden. Add a nice trickling fountain or pond. You can buy a 3ft fountain or make your own DIY solar fountain. To make a DIY solar fountain, like the one above, you will need a barrel. The photo above right shows a resin barrel with a "wooden" design. I purchased a solar fountain pump from Amazon for $20.

Pictured: A lettuce knife for cutting vegetables.

Try to grow a variety of tomatoes. This flavorful mix is sure to be a hit. Put your vegetables on display, and give as many as you can't eat, away. With enough sun, your garden will be plentiful.

Tip: Check your garden every day for ripe vegetables to pull.

Be sure to keep a watering can or a hose. You can also use an irrigation set that will water your garden on a schedule. Irrigation sets today are relatively inexpensive.

The happy gardener *(Right, 2016)* is my husband, at our old townhouse after pulling vegetables from the garden.

You can grow different types of vegetables in small garden beds, planting pots, or grow bags. You can even grow onions, garlic, or fruit like watermelon, cantaloupe, or root vegetables like carrots or potatoes. You can accomplish this whether you are have a patio, backyard, or small area. As you can see from the photos, I have had productive gardens in each of these settings for close to two decades. Even with a large backyard, I prefer to grow veggies on my patio, close to my kitchen door. What a wonderful feeling it is to slide my patio door open to grab a tomato or pepper. Or to go outside and sit for a cool drink before watering the plants. Growing a garden is the highlight of my summer. I enjoy the tranquility and hope you will too.

The final photo of this gardening book is of a rainy spring day in late April. Here, you see the apple tree. It is in full blossom but leaning heavily. Apple trees will produce beautiful apple blossoms that will bear fruit within weeks after the petals fall off. You'll often see these beautiful petals blowing across your yard or in the wind. They look very similar to cherry blossoms. Unfortunately, by mid-summer the tree had fallen. We plan to plant another. We still have a small cherry tree.

I hope this book encourages you to create your own potted garden whether you live in the city, a small apartment, or have limited space. While you're at it, be sure to add flowers, a fountain or other designs to bring peace and a bit of style to your space or garden sanctuary. Enjoy!